Summary

of

The Education of an Idealist

Samantha Power

Conversation Starters

By BookNation

Please Note: This is an unofficial conversation starters guide. If you have not yet read the original work, please do so first. Buy the book here.

Copyright © 2020 by BookNation. All Rights Reserved.
First Published in the United States of America

We hope you enjoy this supplemental guide from BookNation. Our mission is to aid readers and reading groups with quality, thought provoking material to in the discovery and discussions on some of today's favorite books.

Disclaimer / Terms of Use: Product names, logos, brands, and other trademarks featured or referred to within this publication are the property of their respective trademark holders and are not affiliated with BookNation. The publisher and author make no representations or warranties with respect to the accuracy or completeness of these contents and disclaim all warranties such as warranties of fitness for a particular purpose. This guide is unofficial and unauthorized. It is not authorized, approved, licensed, or endorsed by the original book's author or publisher and any of their licensees or affiliates.

No part of this publication may be reproduced or retransmitted, electronic or mechanical, without the written permission of the publisher.

Tips for Using BookNation Conversation Starters:

EVERY GOOD BOOK CONTAINS A WORLD FAR DEEPER THAN the surface of its pages. The characters and their world come alive through the words on the pages, yet the characters and its world still live on. Questions herein are designed to bring us beneath the surface of the page and invite us into the world that lives on. These questions can be used to:

- Foster a deeper understanding of the book
- Promote an atmosphere of discussion for groups
- Assist in the study of the book, either individually or corporately
- Explore unseen realms of the book as never seen before

About Us:

THROUGH YEARS OF EXPERIENCE AND FIELD EXPERTISE, from newspaper featured book clubs to local library chapters, *BookNation* can bring your book discussion to life. Host your book party as we discuss some of today's most widely read books.

Conversation Starters

on

Samantha Power's

The Education of an Idealist

By dailyBooks

About Us:

THROUGH YEARS OF EXPERIENCE AND FIELD EXPERTISE, from newspaper featured book clubs to local library chapters, *dailyBooks* can bring your book discussion to life. Host your book meets as we discuss some of today's most widely read books.

Copyright © 2019 by dailyBooks. All Rights Reserved. Published in the United States of America

Disclaimer: This is an unofficial conversation starters guide. If you have not yet read the original work we encourage you to do so first before reading this Conversation Starters Product names, logos, brands, and other trademarks featured or referred to within this publication are the property of their respective trademark holders and are not affiliated with dailyBooks. The publisher and author make no representations or warranties with respect to the accuracy or completeness of these contents and disclaim all warranties such as warranties of fitness for a particular purpose. This guide is unofficial and unauthorized. It is not authorized, approved, licensed, or endorsed by the original book's author or publisher and any of their licensees or affiliates. No part of this publication may be reproduced or retransmitted, electronic or mechanical, without the written permission of the publisher.

Tips for Using dailyBooks Conversation Starters:

EVERY GOOD BOOK CONTAINS A WORLD FAR DEEPER THAN the surface of its pages. The characters and their world come alive through the words on the pages, yet the characters and their world still live on. Questions herein are designed to bring us beneath the surface of the page and invite us into the world that lives on. These questions can be used to:

- Foster a deeper understanding of the book
- Promote an atmosphere of discussion for groups
- Assist in the study of the book, either individually or corporately
- Explore unseen realms of the book as never seen before

Table of Contents

Introducing The Education of an Idealist

Introducing the Author

Inspiration Behind The Education of an Idealist

Discussion Questions

Quiz Questions

Quiz Answers

Introducing The Education of an Idealist

The Education of an Idealist is a memoir by Samantha Power. The book showed a response from Power to the question "What can one person do?" with a call for people to clearly see, show kindness and have a more open and nationalistic mind. It started with Power's description of her birthplace in Iceland and her time spent as a little girl, reading books in a Dublin Pub where her father held courts upstairs in the bar. Power also mentioned how she and her mother immigrated to America in the 1970s and how she fell in love with the Pittsburgh Pirates and the American idealism. She began to describe her early life and education until the onset of her career in journalism. The narration continued to being noticed by then-Senator for Illinois, Barrack Obama, because of her different ideas and thoughts about the United States foreign policy in 2005. Obama gave her work in the Capitol Hill and on to his presidential campaign. When Obama became president, Power served as Obama's Human Rights Adviser for four years as she tried to put her ideas into practice. She went on from being an outsider activist into the insides of the White House government.

Power brought her idealism to the two successive Obama governance as a Director for Multinational affairs in the National Security Council before being named as the youngest American ambassador for the United Nations in 2013.

One fascinating chapter of the book was when Power worked as a Foreign Policy Adviser of Obama. She was forced to resign from the campaign after she called Obama's rival, Hilary Clinton, a "monster" while she was on a book tour in Ireland. She was just taken back into the position after her friend and another Obama adviser, Richard Holbrooke, gave her the time to have a personal meeting with Clinton to apologize, as a wedding gift.

Power recalled a telephone conversation with Senator McCain in which he criticized her for still giving her support to the President. McCain told her that the president's inaction with regards to the happenings in Syria was a betrayal to the American principles and interests. McCain even shouted at her to resign after telling her that her presence became a crucial task for the government to still pretend as good international citizens.

The book focused on the problems and conflicts between the dictates of the administration and necessary actions to the widespread human suffering. The tension went up to its peak in August 2013. Power has only been serving the United Nations for three weeks when news spread about suspected chemical weapons attack in Damascus, Syria in the early hours of August 21, 2013. An estimated death toll of 1, 429 people including 426 children were reported. The United Nation's investigating team said that sarin gas was used even though the use of chemical weapons has been prohibited by the international norm. Power revealed how the government would have wanted military intervention in Syria right after the attack. Obama said that the use of chemical weapons was the red line for them and enormous consequences shall be given for its continuous usage. Obama instructed the Chairman of the Joint Chiefs of Staff to prepare for airstrikes and told Power to stop the United Nation's mission in Damascus for the meantime. Power said that she received a call from National Security Adviser, Susan Rice, telling her news about the President seeking authorization first from congress for its use of force before giving military strikes to punish the government of Syrian President Bashar al-Assad. After the heated debate on August 30, 2003, the UK-Parliament ruled out joining the US-led strikes with 285 votes to 272. Obama gave out his speech the very next day, saying that he wouldn't act without the authorization from Congress. The opportunity for the Obama administration to intervene in Syria closed for good but the question, "Why did Obama not proceed with the strikes without the congress' authorization?" remains.

Though there were some serious insights and anecdotes from the book, there were also some funny moments. One event that happened was when Power was having a phone conversation with her stepfather who was taking care of her baby. The infant doesn't want to feed on her bottle, making Power's stepfather frustrated. Obama, who was within earshot, grabbed the phone and gave the instructions. After a few minutes, Obama handed the phone back, telling Power that the stepfather already got it.

Power's memoir is partly an autobiography and a political book. It is the story of how Power made people understand her realistic yet ordinary views in life.

Introducing the Author

Samantha Power is an Irish-American activist, academic, author, and policymaker. She was a member of the democratic party and the former 28th United States Ambassador to the United Nations from 2013 to 2017. She started writing the memoir when she was covering the Balkan war as a journalist. She said that it took her ten years to write her book and finished it only after graduating from law school.

The Education of an Idealist was created by Power to put a closure to her painful youth and personal struggles however, after the book's release, the pressure came back. Her childhood battles were scrutinized with the revelations she shared about the Obama administration that were different from her own beliefs.

Before Power entered the government, she only had strong thoughts about how to respond to mass extermination and cruelty. She recalled looking at TV pictures of protestors being crashed by the Chinese government. That was the moment that turned her into a foreign policy advocate from being a sports journalist. At twenty-three, Power went to Bosnia after the mass murder that happened. She met the retired diplomat and Bosnia's President, Morton Abramowitz, who became her mentor and was the one who got her into thinking about what Washington should be doing.

In an interview about her book, Power said that her desires for risks and dangers are getting lesser as she gets older and has a family to worry about. When in a decision to make, she asked herself questions to help her decide which path to take. Questions such as if she'll become more credible when she comes back, or if reading news of what's happening would be good enough, and if she could get new learnings about how to solve differences in a negotiation.

When asked about how America's approach to worldwide crises has changed, Power responded that the use of military force has been tiring and the perception of it to stop the root causes of the crisis was rare. She said that the approach might just be overconfidence and correcting the kind of adventurism it had might be good. She continued by giving an example about preventing Iran to acquire nuclear weapons. She insisted that yelling at them or telling them to be different would not stop Iran from doing so. She said that diplomacy, engagement and foreign policy are required for it. To conclude it all, she said that Americans don't want a war with the middle east again and nor the other way around.

Power's main purpose when creating the book was to call for everyone to act in times of despair. She said that she would like people to feel that they can do something about their problems and that it can be solved. Power's plan is to campaign for a democratic cause in swing states before returning to serve in the government. She stated that the present crises in our world these days need more caring people who are willing to take risks, even though, based on the first lesson from her memoir, putting ourselves online does not always work out.

Inspiration Behind The Education of an Idealist

The Education of an Idealist by Samantha Power was published on September 10, 2019, by HarperCollins, with imprints from Dey Street Books. On November 5, 2019, she had a conversation with Jonathan Freedland at the Guardian Live Event in London for the book. After the book's release, it became a bestseller at New York Times, Wall Street Journal and USA Today.

The book gained lots of praise from readers. First in line was President Barack Obama, who said that the book is a must-read for anyone who cares for each of our roles in a changing world. Colm Toibin, author of Brooklyn and Nora Webster commented that the book contains honest and revealing development of a young woman's inner strength and self-knowledge. According to the New York

Times Book Review by Thomas L. Friedman, Power's memoir interweaves with her personal story, diplomatic history and moral arguments with all honesty while Rachel Maddow from MSNBC adored Power's writing skills, which made the former US official's memoir fun and truly engrossing to read. The Education of an Idealist from The Washington Post's point of view is a moving account of how to serve righteously or at least to try. They continued to note that Power wrote with heart about her upbringing yet it was full of humor and Obama's funniest anecdotes. The Economist review about the book tells the readers of its engaging character and the memoir being an insider's account of foreign policy-making with a personal touch. The Vogue, on the other hand, said that it was Power's turn to be in the international spotlight after writing the book vividly and lucidly. The Independent from Ireland also shared its own review and said that

Power is a master story-teller, who gave a brilliant self-portrait of an outsider turned insider while The Irish Times commented that the memoir gave a riveting fly-on-the insight into the foreign policy decision making during Obama's administration and the inner workings of the United Nations.

While some praised the book, others also gave out unfavorable opinions about it. One reader from Amazon said that he wondered what has gone into Power that made her write the book. He continued that parts of the book were excruciating to read because it seemed like Power kept including herself into every situation, wanting to take some measure of credit. Another criticism came from a book purchaser who said that Power's memoir has a huge blind spot. He said that Power ignored the important link between diversity and genocide because of many differences. He concluded that Power should have included that in the book as she constantly praised the United States for diversity while consistently criticizing various other countries for genocide. One more negative commenter said that the book showed Power's idealist side but implied that Power has been educated to be more of a realist. In conclusion, the quote that gained a lot of negative reviews in Power's new book tells everyone that "We could hardly expect to have a crystal ball when it came to accurately predict outcomes in places where the culture is not our own."

Discussion Questions

question 1

The Education of an Idealist is a memoir by Samantha Power. Do you think the title fits the story? What do you think is the significance of the title in the story? What do you think about the importance of the title in Power's life?

question 2

The book showed a response from Power to the question "What can one person do?". Do you think this question was answered in the book? How do you think did Power answered the question? What were other questions that could be answered in the book?

question 3

Power was noticed by Barrack Obama because of her different ideas and thoughts about the US foreign policy. What do you think about Obama noticing her? Do you think she deserved to be noticed? How do you think did her thoughts and ideas capture the attention of Obama?

question 4

Power called Obama's rival, Hilary Clinton, a "monster". Do you think it was right for her to call Clinton a monster? What do you think made Power call Clinton a monster? How do you think did it affect Power, Obama, and Clinton?

question 5

Power brought her idealism to the two successive Obama governance. Do you think she was successful in doing so? What do you think made her bring her idealism? How do you think did it affect the Obama administration?

question 6

Power is the youngest American ambassador for the United Nations in 2013. Do you think being an ambassador fits her? Do you think she deserved to be appointed as one? What do you think made her deserving?

question 7

Richard Holbrooke gave Power the time to have a personal meeting with Clinton to apologize. What do you think about Power's apology to Clinton? Do you think she should have apologized personally or also in public? Explain your answer.

question 8

McCain told Power that the president's inaction to the happenings in Syria was a betrayal to America. Do you agree with this? Do you think the President should have intervened with what happened to Syria? What do you think the president should have done?

question 9

The book focused on the conflicts between the dictates of the administration and on the human sufferings. Do you think the dictates of the administration differ from the human sufferings? Do you think the book was able to explain the conflicts? How do you think did the book explain it?

question 10

The UN investigating team said that sarin gas was used even though it was already prohibited. What do you think about the usage of sarin gas? Do you think its usage could be prohibited just because it was a policy? How do you think could the usage of chemical gases be surely prohibited?

question 11

Obama said that the use of chemical weapons was the red line and enormous consequences shall be given. Do you agree with what Obama said? Do you think the use of chemical weapons deserves to have consequences? Do you think it was right to give people a warning about the consequences of its usage?

question 12

The President asked for the congress' authorization first before it will use force for military strikes. Do you agree with this? Do you think it was right to ask the congress' authorization first? Do you think the President doesn't have the power to instruct it without the congress' permission?

question 13

The UK-Parliament ruled out joining the US-led strikes with 285 votes to 272. Do you think it was right for the UK-Parliament to join the US-led strikes? What do you think made them agree to join? How do you think did they react when the US-led strikes were not implemented?

question 14

Power was having a phone conversation with her stepfather who was taking care of her baby. What do you think about a stepfather taking care of his stepdaughter's baby? How do you think was Power's relationship with her stepfather? Do you think the baby made them even closer?

question 15

Obama grabbed the phone and gave Power's stepfather the instructions on how to feed the baby. Do you think it was right for Obama to grab Power's phone? What do you think about Obama's intervention? How do you think did Obama made the stepfather understand?

question 16

Power was a member of the democratic party. What do you think made her a member of the democratic party? Do you think she deserved to be a member of the democratic party? How do you think did becoming a member of the democratic party affect Power's idealism views?

question 17

The Education of an Idealist was created by Power to put a closure to her painful youth and personal struggles. Do you think the book released her inner pains? How do you think did the book helped her? Do you think to make the public read about her struggles gave her closure from her past?

question 18

Power said that it took her ten years to write her book. What do you think about the length of time that the book was made? Why do you think did it took a long time for her to write the book? Do you think it was all worth it?

question 19

Power was scrutinized with the revelations she shared about the Obama administration that were different from her own beliefs. Do you think it was good for her to reveal those to the public? What do you think about the revelations? How do you think did the scrutiny of others affects Power?

question 20

Power had strong thoughts about how to respond to mass extermination and cruelty. Do you think it was not that heavy for her to think about those? Do you think she could respond well to mass extermination and cruelty? What do you think is the right way to respond to those?

question 21

At twenty-three, Power went to Bosnia after the mass murder happened. What do you think convinced Power to go to the place where the mass murder happened? Do you think she wasn't too young to go to a dangerous place? How do you think her travel to Bosnia helped her?

question 22

Power said that her desires for risks and dangers are getting lesser as she gets older and has a family. What do you think made her desire less for risks and dangers? Do you think she regretted her actions when she was younger and still has no family? How do you think did her views and principles in life changed now as she's older and has a family?

question 23

Bosnian President, Morton Abramowitz, was the one who made Power think about what Washington should be doing. Do you think Abramowitz was able to help Power become more active with work? How do you think did he changed Power's views and beliefs? What do you think made Power listen to him?

question 24

Power said that correcting the kind of adventurism America had might be good. What do you think about Power's statement about correcting the adventurism in America? Do you think it might be good for America to change it? How do you think Power could change it?

question 25

Power insisted that yelling at Iran or telling them to be different would not stop them from acquiring nuclear weapons. Do you agree with Power? Do you think Iran would be stopped? Do you think America has the right to stop them?

question 26

Power said that diplomacy, engagement and foreign policy are required. Do you think Power is right? How do you think these could help make our world a better place? How do you think Power could implement this?

question 27

Americans don't want a war with the middle east again and so is the other way around. Do you think America doesn't want to have a war with the middle east? Do you think the middle east doesn't want to have a war with America? How do you think will it affect other countries?

question 28

Power's main purpose when creating the book was to call for everyone to act in times of despair. Do you think the book really called out action from everyone? Do you think the book made everyone believe about taking action? How do you think Power's memoir could make the people act in times of despair?

question 29

Power liked people to feel that they can do something about their problems and that it can be solved. Do you think Power made the people feel that way through her book? What do you think about Power's intention? Do you think Power successfully was able to make people feel that way?

question 30

Power stated that the present crises in our world these days need more caring people who are willing to take risks. Do you think the present crises in our world today need more caring people? Do you think people are willing to take risks? What do you think made Power believe in that statement?

question 31

President Barack Obama said that the book is a must-read for anyone who cares for our roles in a changing world. Do you think the book convinced the readers about the different roles that we have in a changing world? How do you think will the book affect somebody? Do you think Obama liked the book?

question 32

Colm Toibin commented that the book contains honest and revealing development of a young woman's inner strength and self-knowledge. What do you think about Power's development in the book? Do you think her development could inspire other people? Do you think the development was a good one?

question 33

The Washington Post said that the book is a moving account of how to serve righteously or at least to try. Do you think the book showed the readers how to serve righteously? Do you agree that it convinced the readers to at least try serving the right way? How were you moved by the contents in the book?

question 34

The power kept including herself into every situation, wanting to take some measure of credit. Do you think Power kept on including herself in every situation in the book? Do you think Power wanted to always take some credit? Should Power not include herself in some situations in her memoir?

question 35

We could hardly expect to have a crystal ball when it came to accurately predict outcomes in places where the culture is not our own. Do you think it is possible for us to guess the outcomes of other countries? What do you think we could do about these places that are not our own? How do you think we could help the counties where the culture is different from ours?

question 36

The Education of an Idealist is a memoir by Samantha Power. How would the story change if the memoir had a different title? What would have happened if the idealist had no education? How would the story be affected if the book was not a memoir but an autobiography?

question 37

The book showed a response from Power to the question "What can one person do?" How do you think the story will change if the question that inspired the story is different? What would happen if Power just wrote her life story without any motivational quotes to follow?

question 38

Power also mentioned how she and her mother immigrated to America in the 1970s. What would have happened if they did not migrate to America? How do you think the story would have changed if they stayed in their place? What would happen if Power didn't learn about America's culture and beliefs before?

question 39

Power was noticed by then-Senator for Illinois, Barrack Obama, because of her different ideas and thoughts about the US foreign policy. What would have happened if Power was not noticed by Obama? How would the story change if Power wasn't determined enough to tell the world about her different thoughts about foreign policy? What would happen if Obama just ignored Power?

question 40

Obama gave her work in the Capitol Hill and on to his presidential campaign. How do you think the story would change if Obama didn't offer Power work? What would happen if Obama didn't include Power to his presidential campaign? How would the story change if Power did not accept Obama's offer for work?

question 41

Power revealed how the government would have wanted military intervention in Syria right after the attack. What would have happened if the government immediately intervened with the happenings in Syria after the attack? How would the story change if Syria continued with its attack? What would happen if Syria attacked the US?

question 42

Power became the youngest American ambassador for the United Nations in 2013. How would the story change if Power wasn't appointed as an ambassador? What would have happened if another person got picked as an ambassador? How do you think the story would change if Power did not accept the offer of becoming an ambassador?

question 43

Richard Holbrooke gave Power the time to have a personal meeting with Clinton to apologize. What do you think would have happened if Power wasn't given the chance to apologize personally? How would the story change if Power apologized publicly instead of personally? What would happen if Power doesn't want to apologize?

question 44

The President asked authorization first from congress for its use of force before giving military strikes. How do you think will the story change if the President just permit the military strikes without the congress' authorization? What would have happened if the congress also gave them permission to do it right away? How will the story change if there were many Americans who died because of the attack? Will the President still not do something about it?

question 45

The UK-Parliament ruled out joining the US-led strikes. What would have happened if The UK-Parliament joined the US-led strikes? What would have happened if the UK-Parliament went on ahead by themselves to attack? How would the story change if the US government had a deal with the UK-Parliament to strike but then the US suddenly backs out from the plan?

Quiz Questions

question 1

The book started with Power's description of her birthplace in ___. She spent her time as a little girl, reading books in a Dublin Pub. Her father held courts upstairs of the pub.

question 2

Power got noticed by then-Senator for Illinois, Barrack Obama, because of her different ideas and thoughts about the United States foreign policy. Obama gave her work in the ___ and on to his presidential campaign. Power served as Obama's Human Rights Adviser when Obama became president.

question 3

Samantha Power is an Irish-American activist, academic, author and policymaker. She was a member of the democratic party. She was the former 28th United States Ambassador to the ____ from 2013 to 2017.

question 4

At twenty-three, Power went to ___ after the mass murder that happened. She met the retired diplomat and Bosnia's President, Morton Abramowitz. Abramowitz became her mentor and was the one who got her into thinking about what Washington should be doing?

question 5

According to the New York Times Book Review by Thomas L. Friedman, Power's memoir interweaves with her personal story. It narrated her ____ history and moral arguments with all honesty while Rachel Maddow from MSNBC adored Power's writing skills, which made the former US official's memoir fun and truly engrossing to read.

question 6

Another criticism came from a book purchaser who said that Power's memoir has a huge blind spot. He said that Power ignored the important link between ____ and genocide. He concluded that Power should have included that in the book.

question 7

True or False: The Education of an Idealist is a memoir by Samantha Power. The book showed a response from Power to the question "What can one person do?" with a call for people to clearly see, show kindness and have a more open and nationalistic mind.

question 8

True or False: Obama gave out his speech, saying that he would act even without the authorization from congress. Since then, he gave instructions to attack Syria with airstrikes. The opportunity for the Obama administration to intervene in Syria ended after the war.

question 9

True or False: The Education of an Idealist was created by Power to put a closure to her painful youth and personal struggles. After the book's release, though, the pressure came back. Her childhood battles were scrutinized with the revelations she shared in the book.

question 10

True or False: In an interview about her book, Power said that her desires for risks and dangers are increasing as she gets older. She wanted to protect her family by standing on her own ideas. When in a decision to make, she asked herself questions to help her decide which path to take.

question 11

True or False: The Education of an Idealist from The Washington Post's point of view is a moving account of how to serve righteously or at least to try. They continued to note that Power wrote with heart about her upbringing. It was a book full of humor and Obama's funniest anecdotes.

question 12

True or False: One reader from Amazon said that he understands what has gone into Power that made her write the book. He continued that parts of the book were good to read because it seemed like Power wanted to do something in every situation.

Quiz Answers

1. Iceland
2. Capitol Hill
3. United Nations
4. Bosnia
5. Diplomatic
6. Diversity
7. True
8. False
9. True
10. False
11. True
12. False

THANK YOU

YOUR VOICE MATTERS.
PLEASE LEAVE A REVIEW.

If you enjoyed this book and it has helped you, we'd love to hear from you.

Bonus Downloads

*Get Free Books with **Any Purchase** of* Conversation Starters

Every purchase comes with a FREE download!

Get it Now

or Click Here.

Scan Your Phone

Made in the USA
Middletown, DE
07 March 2021